P&O Port Out, Starboard Home

David L. Williams

Ian Allan 60th ANNIVERSARY

Front cover: Though completed in 1960 for the Orient Line by Vickers Armstrong at Barrow-in-Furness, the 41,930-gross-ton *Oriana* essentially entered service as a P&O-Orient ship as the amalgamation of her original owner with P&O had occurred in May of that year. She adopted the P&O colours of white hull and yellow funnels from 1964. Along with the contemporary *Canberra*, the *Oriana* represented both a radical departure from the style and layout of previous liners introduced on the Australia mail run and a quite significant jump in size for ships employed on this route, of the order of 30%. Her principal dimensions were 804ft (245.1m) overall length and 97ft (29.6m) beam.
Bettina Rohbrecht

Back cover: The *Pride of Portsmouth* is one of two large passenger/car ferries operating on P&O European Ferries' Portsmouth to Le Havre service. She was built by Schichau Seebeckwerft AG at Bremerhaven as the *Olau Britannia* for Olau Line (UK), making her entry into the Flushing to Sheerness service on 21 May 1990. With her sister-ship *Olau Hollandia*, renamed *Pride of Le Havre*, she transferred to P&O in 1994, the arrangement being an extended charter rather than an outright purchase. The pair brought significantly improved standards of passenger accommodation and greater spaciousness to the longer cross-Channel route. The majority of the cabins have private facilities. The *Pride of Portsmouth* measures 33,336 gross tons. She is 528ft (160.9m) long with a beam of 95ft (29.0m).
Bettina Rohbrecht

Title page: Second of the Princess Cruises' 'Grand Princess'-class, the *Golden Princess* is shown berthed in one of the European ports she visited on her pre-service promotional tour, prior to her departure for warmer climes.
Bettina Rohbrecht

Acknowledgements

In appreciation of the assistance I have received in the preparation of this book, I should like to acknowledge the following companies and individuals:

John Edgington, Christine Fisher, Mike Louagie, Meyer Werft (Jos. L. Meyer GmbH), P&O Cruises, P&O European Ferries (Portsmouth) — Gary Williams, P&O North Sea Ferries — Philip van Wijnen, P&O Steam Navigation Co — Stephen Rabson and Sue Cox, David Reed, Philip Rentell, Bettina Rohbrecht, Ian Shiffman, Don Smith, the late Ray Sprake, World Ship Society.

Bibliography

Haws, Duncan; *Merchant Fleets in Profile, No 1 — P&O, Orient & Blue Anchor Lines*; Patrick Stephens, 1978.
Kludas, Arnold; *Great Passenger Ships of the World, Volumes 1-6*; Patrick Stephens, 1974-86.
Kludas, Arnold; *Great Passenger Ships of the World Today*; Patrick Stephens, 1992.
Miller, William H., Jr; *Picture History of British Ocean Liners, 1900 to the Present*; Dover Publications, 2001.
Smith, Eugene W.; *Passenger Ships of the World, Past & Present*; George H. Dean, 1963.
Williams, David L.; *Cruise Ships*; Ian Allan Publishing, 2001.
Williams, David L.; *Glory Days: P&O*; Ian Allan Publishing, 1999.
Williams, David L.; *Wartime Disasters at Sea*; Patrick Stephens, 1997.

plus numerous issues of Lloyd's Register of Shipping, *Sea Lines* (the magazine of the Ocean Liner Society), *Marine News* (the journal of the World Ship Society) and *Cruise Ferry Notes*.

First published 2002

ISBN 0 7110 2850 8

© Ian Allan Publishing Ltd 2002

Published by Ian Allan Publishing

an imprint of Ian Allan Publishing Ltd, Hersham, Surrey KT12 4RG.
Printed by Ian Allan Printing Ltd, Hersham, Surrey KT12 4RG.

Code: 0209/B3

Introduction

The word 'posh' has been attributed apocryphally to travel aboard P&O steamers during the Victorian era, alluding to their furnace-like interiors in the heat of the tropics, before the days of air-conditioning, and the relative relief that could be enjoyed in those cabins on the shaded side of the ship — on the port side when travelling eastwards and on the starboard side for the return voyage. Hence: Port Out — Starboard Home, abbreviated to 'POSH'.

Whether or not there is any truth in this story is impossible to determine and is largely irrelevant anyway for, rightly or wrongly, many people now believe this to be the word's origin and in a sense it is a justified assumption. We commonly associate the word 'posh' with places and behaviour of an impeccable standard, to do with things that are luxurious, grand and enjoyed by a select minority. For much of its 165-year history from its foundation in 1837, P&O has been striving to achieve these very qualities aboard the ships of its fleet, though not quite so ostentatiously, and it pioneered or adopted numerous developments and improvements to ensure that they were the most comfortable and spacious ships on their routes, as well as being the safest and fastest vessels on which to take an ocean passage.

Using colour pictures throughout, this book traces the history of P&O's passenger shipping enterprise from its earliest days. It follows its ascendancy from modest beginnings into one of the greatest passenger shipping companies of all time. The picture section — a gallery of the company's vessels in the post-World War 2 period — completes the story, tracking P&O's progress over a period of dynamic change with a narrative which concentrates on the ships' particulars and achievements.

It all began, according to the company's archives, back in 1815 with the start of a long association between Brodie McGhee Willcox, who opened a shipbroking office in Lime Street, London, and Arthur Anderson, whom Willcox engaged as his clerk. The company's main business was the operation of sailing ships on passages to the Iberian peninsula, acting as the agents for various owners. A feature of the operation was the establishment, as far as possible, of a regular schedule of sailings.

By 1822, the association between Willcox and Anderson had developed into a partnership. Eleven years later, they chartered the first ships to run under their own name, notably the *William Fawcett* (206 tons burthen; 82ft/25.0m length), owned by the Dublin & London Steam Packet Company, which is regarded as the very first P&O ship. Other early vessels which made sailings for Willcox & Anderson were the *Royal Tar*, *City of Londonderry* and *Liverpool*.

The operation was so successful that just three years after its inception, the company took delivery of the very first new ship built to its own account, the *Iberia* (516 gross tons; 155ft/47.2m length), followed by the similar *Braganza*. Essentially, the introduction of this pair of modestly sized paddle steamships marked the founding of the Peninsular Steam Navigation Company, as it was first known.

Long before P&O came to be associated with ocean cruises, the *Iberia*, along with other early P&O ships, featured in a pioneering excursion trip in 1844, which was effectively the very first Mediterranean cruise. Among the noted passengers who embarked for that inaugural leisure tour was the English writer William Makepeace Thackeray who recorded the experience for posterity in his *Notes of a Journey from Cornhill to Grand Cairo*. Already P&O was attracting a reputation for the high quality of its shipboard accommodation, for the *Iberia* was described as the finest ship afloat.

With its new ships, the company was able to offer regular departures destined for Vigo, Oporto, Lisbon, Cadiz and Gibraltar, with onward connections to Malta and Corfu. Monthly links to Alexandria and an overland journey to Port Suez permitted onward travel to India aboard ships owned by other shipping lines.

Having itself secured the Indian mail contract in 1839, the board of the company agreed to its being renamed the Peninsular & Oriental Steam Navigation Company from 23 April 1840. Soon, of course, it was more commonly referred to as the P&O Line.

From this date, P&O progressively secured more mail-carrying contracts across a rapidly expanding route network: from Bombay to Madras, Calcutta and Ceylon (Sri Lanka) in 1842; to Penang, Singapore and Hong Kong in 1844; to Shanghai five years later and to Australia in 1852, when the first *Chusan* inaugurated a twice-monthly mail service to Sydney.

East of Suez, P&O introduced its own ships from 1842, the wooden-hulled *Hindostan* and *Bentinck* (2,018 gross tons; 218ft/66.4m length) built by Thomas Wilson & Co, Liverpool, each making its positioning voyage around the Cape of Good Hope. Both were significantly larger than P&O's previous largest ship, the chartered 1,300-ton *Great Liverpool*. Some 18 years prior to the opening of the Suez Canal (the incredible feat of construction inspired by Ferdinand de Lesseps which permitted direct navigation from the Mediterranean to the Red Sea), it was still essential for the passengers to cross the isthmus by slow and primitive transportation, a journey of 100 hours' duration. In 1851 work commenced on a rail link which significantly reduced the transit time while simultaneously offering through-passengers improved standards of comfort for the journey.

P&O had largely established the full extent of its route structure by the mid-19th century, and the next 50 years or more witnessed a steady improvement to the P&O fleet with the introduction of bigger, faster and more commodious vessels.

P&O's earliest steamers were wooden-hulled but in 1842 it took delivery of its first iron-hulled ship, the 548-gross-ton *Pacha*. Likewise, paddle propulsion was the vogue until the 1850s, from when the company progressively switched to propeller-driven vessels, beginning with the first *Shanghai* of 1851. The last paddle vessel to join the P&O Line fleet was the *Nyanza* (2,082 gross tons; 327ft/99.7m length) completed by the Thames Iron Works in November 1864. Thereafter, all new passenger ships were fitted with screw propellers. The adoption of technical innovations was also evident in other facilities and fittings installed within the ships. As they became available, piped hot water, electric lighting, radio telegraphy, refrigerated storage, air-conditioning and stabilisation, to name just the more obvious innovations, were swiftly adopted by P&O.

Passenger ships in general grew rapidly in size over the course of the 19th century and well into the 20th century, leading to ships that eventually dwarfed those that had pioneered the ocean steamship routes. This was as true of P&O as it was of other shipping lines whose business was in other oceans.

A major step forward in size was taken with the *Himalaya*, completed in December 1853, which was acknowledged for her elegant lines. Though she had a long life, surviving to the 1940s, she did not remain with P&O for long.

Built by C. J. Mare at Blackwall, she was taken over by the Government as a Crimean war troopship soon after completion and, found to be an excellent vessel, was retained beyond the end of that conflict. Measuring 3,438 gross tons and 372ft (113.4m) in length, she was not

Above: The second *Himalaya* entered the London to Sydney service on 6 January 1893. She was P&O's largest and fastest ship at the time, at 6,898 gross tons, and capable of a speed of 18 knots. Indeed, she broke the England to Australia speed record, via Suez, in her first season, making the voyage in 36½ days. Her sister was the *Australia*, also second of the name. Like so many of the P&O ships entering service in this period, both the *Himalaya* and *Australia* were built by Caird & Company, Greenock. The *Himalaya* had an overall length of 466ft (142.0m) and measured 52ft (15.8m) across her beam. Her draught of 26ft was the maximum permitted at that time for navigation through the Suez Canal. She could accommodate 450 passengers in two classes. Her crew numbered 320. From 1908 she was transferred to the India service, making occasional voyages on the Far East routes. On the outbreak of World War 1 she was taken over for duties as an armed merchant cruiser, converted at Penang and employed to patrol the Red Sea. In June 1916 the Admiralty purchased her outright and had her fitted with a flightdeck to permit the operation of a squadron of seaplanes. P&O repurchased the *Himalaya* in 1919 but she was employed only as a troopship on behalf of the Ministry of Transport until broken up in 1922. *Philip Rentell*

exceeded in size until the emergence of the *Deccan* in 1868 and the second *Hindostan* in the following year.

The 1878-built *Kaiser-I-Hind*, constructed for the Indian services, was P&O's first passenger liner to have a hull of over 400ft (122.0m) in

P. & O. S.S. EGYPT" LEAVING MARSEILLES.
(8,000 TONS, 11,000 HORSE-POWER).

Above: The third ship of the five-ship 'India' class, the *Egypt* alternated between the India and Australia services from August 1897, when she was delivered to P&O. Another vessel from the Caird & Company shipyard, the 7,912-gross-ton *Egypt*, with an overall length of 500ft (152.4m), had five passenger decks with accommodation for 525 passengers in First and Second Class, plus 2,500 troops. The *Egypt* was selected in 1910 to act as Royal Yacht for the homeward voyage from Egypt of HRH The Princess Royal. Following wartime service as Hospital Ship No 52, in which capacity she served in the Mediterranean in support of the Gallipoli forces, the *Egypt* hit the headlines after the return of peace, on 20 May 1922, when she sank off Ushant following a collision in fog with the French steamship *Seine*. She was bound for Marseilles, carrying 338 persons of whom 86 — 15 passengers and 71 crew — were killed. The French vessel was the offender, travelling too fast for the conditions, whereas the *Egypt* had been hove to at the time of the impact. So serious was her damage that the *Egypt* sank, taking with her gold bullion valued at the time at £1,054,000. This became the subject of a spectacular salvage feat carried out by an Italian diving team between 1930 and 1933. The battered but still seaworthy *Seine* conveyed the *Egypt's* survivors to Brest. *Philip Rentell*

length. She was the product of Caird & Co, Greenock, which became the builder of the majority of P&O's new passenger vessels completed from the late 19th century through to World War 1. P&O's first vessels to measure over 5,000 gross tons were introduced in 1881, being the *Rome* and *Carthage*, built for the London to Bombay service. The *Rome* was the first P&O ship to operate from Gravesend on the River Thames. The small *Ravenna* of 1880 (3,372 gross tons; 380ft/115.9m length) was P&O's first steel-hulled ship, followed by the *Clyde*, the first of the five 'River' class liners. Continuing development led to the famed 'Jubilee' class, so called to commemorate Queen Victoria's Golden Jubilee. It comprised four ships delivered between 1887 and 1888, named *Victoria*, *Britannia*, *Oceana* and *Arcadia*.

The next milestone in the development of the P&O fleet was the 'India' class of five vessels, which entered service from 1896. At 7,900 gross tons and 500ft (152.4m) length, they were larger, longer and faster than any of their predecessors. Three were lost in World War 1 — the *India*, *Arabia* and *Persia* — and the *Egypt* became the subject of an incredible salvage feat to recover gold bullion after she foundered following a collision in May 1922. The *Caledonia* of 1894 (7,588 gross tons; 486ft/148.1m length), the first P&O ship to operate from Tilbury Docks, briefly introduced the white hull and yellow funnel colouring by which P&O ships would eventually come to be instantly recognised, an experiment repeated in 1908 with the *Salsette*, a fast ship employed on the Aden to Bombay shuttle service. The *Caledonia* herself was a speedy vessel, breaking the London to Calcutta record with a run of 24 days and 21 hours.

From the early years of the 20th century, P&O began to operate its very first dedicated cruise ship, the *Vectis*, the former *Rome* which had entered the Bombay service back in 1881.

H.M. TRANSPORT "PLASSY" (P & O.) AT ADEN.
(7,500 TONS, 7,000 HORSE-POWER.)

Left: Constructed as one of a trio of troopers by Caird & Company, Greenock, the *Plassy* entered service in December 1900. She measured 7,405 gross tons, with a length of 450ft (137.2m) and beam of 54ft (16.5m). After spending virtually her entire career engaged in Government troop-carrying, both in peacetime and wartime, the *Plassy* was sold for breaking up in Italy in July 1924.
Philip Rentell

She had been reconstructed in 1892, increasing her length to 449ft (136.9m) and raising her tonnage to 5,545 gross tons. From May 1904 the *Vectis* made cruise trips to Northern Europe and the Mediterranean, with shore excursions organised by Thomas Cook.

Following the use of the *Himalaya* of 1853 as a Crimean War troopship, P&O became involved in the transportation of troops to the outposts of the Empire on behalf of the Ministry of Transport, commissioning new ships designed expressly for the purpose. In 1895 the *Simla*, *Nubia* and *Malta*, each of around 6,000 gross tons and 430ft (131.1m) overall length, were introduced. Less than five years later a larger and improved trio of peacetime troopers, the *Assaye*, *Sobraon* and *Plassy*, were delivered to P&O. These later vessels measured 7,405 gross tons and had a length of 450ft (137.2m).

Between 1901 and 1913 P&O embarked upon a major new-building programme, the like of which had never been seen before: five 6,500-gross-ton 'S' class, eight 6,500-gross-ton 'N' class, five 7,500-gross-ton 'P' class, ten 10–12,000-gross-ton 'M' class and four 8,000-gross-ton 'D' class ships. With five 'B' class vessels for the former Lund & Co 'Branch-Line' service via Cape Town, there were in total 37 new ships for the India, Australia and Far East routes. Units of the 'M' class yet again broke size and length records, the *Moldavia* being the first to exceed 500ft in overall length and the *Marmora* being the first P&O ship of over 10,000 gross tons. In fact, the 'M' ships ranged in size from 9,505 to 12,430 gross tons, with dimensions of 530ft to 562ft (161.5m to 171.3m) overall length. The *Medina*, the last ship of the group, was famed for her selection to serve as

Royal Yacht for the visit to India of King George V and Queen Mary in 1911.

If the 19th century had seen the establishment of the P&O Line and the consolidation of its position as the major British shipping line serving Australasia, the Indian subcontinent and the Far East, then the 20th century was characterised by the rise of the P&O Group, as the company grew into a shipping concern of global magnitude and importance. It was a process of dynamic growth but also of acquisition and amalgamation, as the following list, covering the first half of the 20th century, reveals:

1910: acquired the Blue Anchor Line (Lund & Co)
1914: acquired the Australian United Steam Navigation Co and amalgamated with the British India Line
1916: acquired the New Zealand Shipping Co and the Federal Steam Navigation Co
1917: acquired the Union Steamship Co of New Zealand, the Nourse Line and the Hain Steamship Co

1919: acquired the Eastern & Australian Mail Steamship Co and the Khedivial Mail Line (sold in 1924)
1920: acquired the General Steam Navigation Co
1935: acquired the Moss Hutchison Line
1936: acquired the New Medway Steam Packet Co

The fleet expansion and ship development programme that P&O had initiated from the start of the 20th century was soon resumed after World War 1. The most recent prewar ship, the second *Kaiser-I-Hind* (11,518 gross tons, 540ft/164.6m length), which had entered the Bombay service only on 27 June 1914, was chartered to the Cunard Line for six months' operation on the Atlantic service from Southampton to New York, briefly adopting the anglicised version of her name, *Emperor of India*. On her return to P&O she accomplished a record passage from Plymouth to Bombay via Suez, making the run in 17 days, 20 hours and 52 minutes at an average speed of 18.5 knots. Two other ships, planned for entry into service before the outbreak of hostilities, finally came out in 1919/20. They were the three-funnelled 16,500-gross-ton, 605ft (184.4m)-long *Naldera* and *Narkunda*. Within two years, two improved twin-funnelled liners of over 20,000 gross tons had joined them, the *Mooltan* and *Maloja*.

Although P&O rapidly adopted new shipboard, mechanical and navigational innovations, in order to provide its passengers with maximum comfort and convenience, it was not generally regarded as a ground-breaker in pioneering radical changes. However, this image was to be challenged in the period between the wars when P&O commissioned the turbo-electric *Viceroy of India* (19,648 gross tons; 612ft/186.5m overall length), the first British merchant ship to have this propulsion system, followed by the similarly engined *Strathnaver* and *Strathaird*. P&O later returned to turbo-electric drive for the *Canberra*

of 1961, a classic ship which also had a radical engines-aft layout. The first 'Strath' pair were famed for reintroducing the white hull and yellow funnel tropical livery. (This time it was retained for the Australia-run ships and ultimately for the entire P&O fleet.) Known as the 'White Sisters', they were distinguished from the later vessels of this class by having — as built — three bright

Above: P&O had first contracted Harland & Wolff for the construction of the *China*, completed in 1896. It went back to the Belfast shipbuilder for the second pair of the 'M' class, introduced from 1903, one of which was the 10,512-gross-ton *Macedonia*. Launched on 11 April 1903, she commenced her maiden voyage from London to Bombay on 12 February 1904. In 1907 the *Macedonia* transferred to the London to China route. Naval service in World War 1 as an auxiliary cruiser, from August 1914, was followed by troop transportation duties from 1915. While serving as an armed merchant cruiser in the South Atlantic, the *Macedonia*, along with HMS *Bristol*, acted as support ship during the Battle of the Falklands. It is reported that, between them, they sank Admiral Von Spee's supply ships *Baden* and *Santa Isabel* at the time of the action in December 1914. The *Macedonia* remained with the Admiralty until 1921 when she was returned to P&O and refitted in preparation for the resumption of passenger service on the Far East routes. She was broken up in Japan in 1931. *Philip Rentell*

yellow funnels, although the retention of black hulls and funnels had been contemplated, as revealed in postcards released before their completion.

The interwar decades saw no fewer than 27 vessels of postwar design enter service with P&O. Apart from the *Mooltan* and *Maloja*, there were five improved ships for the 'Branch-Line' service, plus the *Moldavia, Mongolia, Razmak, Cathay, Comorin, Chitral, Ranpura, Ranchi, Rawalpindi, Rajputana, Viceroy of India, Strathnaver, Strathaird, Carthage, Corfu, Strathmore, Stratheden, Strathallan, Ettrick* and *Canton*.

World War 2 cost the P&O fleet dearly but yet another rebuilding programme was embarked upon from the late 1940s to make good the losses. The widening and deepening of the Suez Canal permitted the introduction of larger vessels of greater beam and draught. Thus, there were fewer replacement vessels but of much greater tonnage and passenger capacity — the *Himalaya, Arcadia* and *Iberia* for the Australian mail service, the first P&O liners of over 700ft (213.3m) in length with tonnages approaching 30,000 gross tons, and, for the India and Far East services, the 24,000-gross-ton *Chusan*. The crowning glory was the 45,000-gross-ton *Canberra* introduced in 1961, which excelled as both a route liner and a cruise ship.

P&O and the Orient Line had organised their services in a complementary fashion since before World War 2 and had formed the joint Orient & Pacific Line in 1958 for a trans-Pacific service. The full-scale merger of the two companies in 1960, to form P&O-Orient Lines, brought five more large ocean liners into the joint fleet, the *Orion, Orcades, Oronsay, Orsova* and *Oriana* (the *Orontes* was sold almost immediately), the *Oriana* being almost as large as the *Canberra*. In October 1966, the company name reverted to P&O Line, the former Orient ships having already discarded their 'biscuit'-coloured livery for the white and yellow of P&O.

The years that followed witnessed the rapid decline of the regular service line voyages and a gradual transition to full-time cruise operations. It was during this period that the P&O ocean passenger shipping business of today was shaped. Central to this was the acquisition of Princess Cruises (the famed *Love Boat* cruise operators) in 1974.

Simultaneously, P&O entered the coastal passenger ferry business around the British Isles, first through affiliations and subsequently through a series of takeovers. The long-standing group

P. & O. S.S. "MANTUA" OFF COLOMBO. (11,500 TONS, 15,000 HORSE-POWER.)

Above: Seventh ship of the 'M' class was the *Mantua*, for which P&O went back to Caird & Company. She made her maiden voyage from London to Sydney on 4 June 1909. Her dimensions were 562ft (171.3m) length overall and 61ft (18.6m) beam. Tonnage was 10,885 gross tons. The *Mantua* spent the period from 1913 until the outbreak of World War 1 engaged on a programme of luxury cruises (taking over this role from the *Vectis*). Indeed, she was recalled from the last of these, a cruise to the Baltic, in early August 1914 because of the danger of war breaking out. Like many of her class she was taken over for Admiralty service as an armed merchant cruiser, in her case attached to the 10th Cruiser Squadron. From 1915 she became a troopship. After her postwar refit, the *Mantua* returned to the London to Sydney service, calling *en route* at Bombay. As the last surviving unit of the celebrated 'M' class at the time of her disposal, she went to Shanghai ship-breakers in May 1935. *Christine Fisher*

P. & O. Electric Ship STRATHAIRD, 22,500 TONS.
Carrying First-class and Tourist-class Passengers.
India and Australia Mail Service.

Left: P&O upgraded the Australian express mail service yet again with two distinctive new liners delivered in 1931 and 1932, the *Strathnaver* and *Strathaird*, both built by Vickers Armstrong at Barrow-in-Furness. They adopted the propulsion system pioneered three years earlier with the *Viceroy of India* but they were somewhat larger at approximately 22,500 gross tons with an overall length of 664ft (202.4m) and a beam measurement of 80ft (24.4m). This postcard image depicts the new *Strathaird*, the second ship of the pair. *David Williams collection*

Author's Note
The aim of this book is to provide a pictorial history of P&O's passenger shipping services, highlighting their broad scope today. In doing this, I have concentrated on the ships from the P&O Line and P&O Cruises fleets as well as other Group passenger vessels, of all types, which have displayed the P&O logo as part of their livery. This has meant that passenger ships of British India and certain other P&O Group companies from the past have been omitted from this album, whereas the passenger ferries of various P&O short-sea operations have been included. Also, until its demerger from P&O Steam Navigation, on 23 October 2000, it is understood that the Princess Cruises subsidiary, whose ships are an obvious presence in this book, functioned rather less independently than did the British India Line and other Group passenger lines from the scheduled service era.

subsidiary, General Steam Navigation, joined with German and Dutch partners to found North Sea Ferries in 1965. Two years later a similar consortium was formed with the French concern S.A.G.A. and an Irish partner as Normandy Ferries, operating cross-Channel services from Southampton to Le Havre with the *Dragon* and *Leopard*. On the other side of the world, another P&O company, Union Steamship, was pioneering ro-ro services across the Cook Strait.

The P&O European & Air Transport Division was formed in 1971, with P&O Short Sea Shipping acting as manager of its fleet. Around the same time, General Steam Navigation acquired the Coast Lines group, along with its subsidiaries the Belfast Steamship Company and Burns & Laird Lines, extending P&O's ferry operations into the Irish Sea. Ultimately, all these

diverse services became wholly owned by P&O, identified collectively as P&O Ferries.

Today P&O is as renowned for its ferry services, with some of the largest short-sea ships afloat, as it is for its worldwide cruise activities. The passenger shipping side of its business is maintained by numerous cruise and ferry companies, all flying the P&O banner, but as a measure of its enormous involvement in world shipping of all categories the P&O Group today also has a major presence in bulk cargo, container cargo and general cargo shipping. While this book focuses on the passenger side of P&O's diverse operations, it is nevertheless a tribute to P&O's growth in all areas of operations from its small beginnings, some 185 years ago, into a great British commercial concern and institution.

In 1925, P&O placed three new, modestly sized liners on the intermediate service to Sydney, Australia via Bombay, Colombo and Melbourne, these being the *Cathay*, *Comorin* and *Chitral*. So successful were they that two more ships of similar size and dimensions, the *Corfu* and *Carthage*, were ordered for the Far East route. They entered service in 1931. Unlike the earlier trio, which had quadruple-expansion reciprocating engines, the later pair was equipped with Parsons geared turbines,

being only the third and fourth P&O ships to have this type of propulsion machinery, behind the *Moldavia* (1922) and *Mongolia* (1923). Later, in October 1938, the slightly larger *Canton*, measuring 15,784 gross tons and having dimensions of 568ft (173.2m) length and 73.5ft (22.4m) beam, was added to the pair on the Far East services. The fourth ship of the name, the *Canton* entered service painted in P&O's traditional colours of black hull and funnel. After wartime service as an

armed merchant cruiser and a troopship, the *Canton* resumed P&O commercial service in 1946, following a major refit, wearing the company's new tropical livery of white hull and yellow funnel, as shown here. The career of the *Canton* ended in October 1962 when she was sold for scrapping at Hong Kong. The photograph was taken in London on 9 April 1956. *Ian Shiffman*

Following arduous troopship duties performed throughout World War 2, the *Strathaird* emerged from her postwar refit with only a single, central funnel, the dummy forward and aft structures having been removed. The *Strathaird* and *Strathnaver* maintained the Australian front-line service with the new *Himalaya* during the early 1950s, but after the *Arcadia* and *Iberia* were commissioned, in 1954, they were converted to single-class ships focused on the emigrant trade. Originally providing for 500 First Class and 670 Tourist Class passengers, their accommodation layout was modified to give them a capacity of 1,240 all-Tourist Class berths. After making her final round trip to Australia from March to April 1961, the *Strathaird* was sold for breaking up in Hong Kong. Her sister-ship *Strathnaver* suffered the same fate nine months later, in April 1962. *Don Smith*

Above: The *Strathaird* seen in her postwar colours at Tilbury. *World Ship Society*

Right: The three later 'Strath' class ships were completed with only a single funnel and the company also reverted to steam turbines for their main propulsion machinery. All three were built at Barrow by Vickers Armstrong. The *Strathmore*, which made her maiden voyage on the London to Australia express service on 4 October 1935, was slightly different from the later duo and could be identified from them externally by her shorter funnel. She measured 23,580 gross tons. Her dimensions were broadly the same as the first two 'Straths', with only a modest increase in her beam measurement. Less than four years after she entered service, the *Strathmore* was taken over for wartime troop carrying, duties she continued to perform for almost nine years. She resumed her P&O commercial career with her first postwar sailing on 27 October 1949. Twelve years later, in 1961, she was converted into a one-class Tourist ship, continuing in the Sydney service — with the omission of the Bombay call — until June 1963. Then, acquired by the Greek shipowner John S. Latsis, she was placed on the Muslim pilgrim trade between Karachi and Mecca under the name *Marianna Latsis*. Later, she swapped names with her former half-sister, *Stratheden*, becoming the *Henrietta Latsis* from 1966. Three years later she was scrapped at La Spezia, Italy. *Don Smith*

Left: Completing the five-ship 'Strath' series were the *Stratheden*, whose maiden voyage to Australia commenced on 24 December 1937 (the major event of P&O's centenary year), and the *Strathallan*, which made her maiden sailing on 13 March 1938. Their funnels were taller, by 9ft, to help keep the afterdecks clean. The *Strathallan* was a casualty of World War 2, being another loss suffered during the North African landings. P&O lost a total of four vessels in this campaign, the others being the *Cathay*, *Narkunda* and *Viceroy of India*. The *Strathallan* fell victim to an enemy submarine, being torpedoed and sunk off Oran on 22 December 1942. The *Stratheden* survived the war, working throughout as a troopship. By the time she was released by the Ministry of War Transport, in July 1946, she had transported 150,000 troops and had travelled 468,000 miles, taking her from the United Kingdom to South Africa, India, Australia, the Middle East, Norway, the United States and Canada. Following postwar reconditioning, the *Stratheden* re-entered the Australia express service in 1947. Three years later she was chartered to Cunard to fill in on the summer peak season, making four Atlantic round voyages. In 1961, after a further 10 years on the Australia run, her accommodation for 527 First Class and 453 Tourist Class passengers was downgraded to a single class for around 1,200 passengers. At the end of her time in the Australia scheduled service, in August 1963, she was chartered to the Travel Savings Association for a programme of affordable cruises. The following year she joined her former half-sister *Strathmore* as a pilgrim ship, first named *Henrietta Latsis* and then *Marianna Latsis*, the reason for this seemingly pointless swapping of names being unknown. The *Stratheden*, like the *Strathmore*, was broken up at La Spezia in 1969. *Don Smith*

Above: The *Stratheden* on the River Thames at Tilbury on 27 April 1955. *Ian Shiffman*

Above: Launched by Lady Currie, wife of the P&O Chairman, on 5 October 1948, P&O's first new passenger liner commissioned after World War 2 was the *Himalaya*, completed by Vickers Armstrong, Barrow-in-Furness, in 1949. The progressive deepening of the Suez Canal permitted P&O to introduce yet larger ships on the Australia and Far East services. Consequently, although she was developed from the earlier 'Strath' series, the *Himalaya* was a far superior ship, representing a significant increase in size, at 27,955 gross tons, and with improved passenger amenities. She was one of the first P&O ships to be partially air-conditioned (it was later extended to the entire ship during a winter refit) and she was the first big liner to be entirely self-

supporting for her fresh water supplies, having onboard evaporators capable of a daily output of 300 tons of water. Her décor and appointments were sumptuous, matched only by those of the newest Orient Line ships, which, by that time, were operating in close synchronisation with their P&O equivalents. Cabin space aboard the *Himalaya* provided for 743 First Class and 483 Tourist Class passengers. She measured 709ft (216.1m) length overall, 90.5ft (27.6m) across her beam and had a draught of 31ft (9.4m). With a service speed of 22.5 knots, the *Himalaya* cut the London to Melbourne passage time from 32 to 28 days. In 1958 she became the first P&O liner to enter the extended trans-Pacific service operated jointly with Orient Line.

Instead of turning around at Sydney, she continued across the Pacific to San Francisco, returning via the Panama Canal to London, where she arrived on 2 June 1958. Her circumnavigation of the Earth, a total distance of 40,111 miles, was the longest peacetime passage in the history of P&O up to that time. From 1963 the *Himalaya* replaced the last of the 'Straths' in the one-class Tourist service to Australia. In her later years she spent the majority of the time cruising. She sailed into Hong Kong for the last time in November 1974, after which she went to Kaohsiung, Taiwan, for breaking up. Here, the *Himalaya* is seen in Southampton Water a few months earlier, in May 1974. *Ian Shiffman*

Previous page and above: Similar to the *Himalaya*, but smaller, was the Vickers Armstrong-built *Chusan*, which entered the UK to Far East service in September 1950. The *Chusan* measured 24,570 gross tons with dimensions of 672.5ft (205.0m) length overall and 85ft (25.9m) beam. She could accommodate 464 First Class and 541 Tourist Class passengers. On her second voyage, in November 1950, the *Chusan* became the first British passenger ship to resume calls at Japanese ports after World War 2 when she made her first call at Yokohama. An unusual feature of both the *Chusan* from 1951 and the *Himalaya* from 1953 was the Thornycroft cowl that was fitted to the funnel of each ship, designed to reduce the nuisance of smoke smuts falling on the aft passenger decks. The *Chusan* continued in the Far East service until 1959 when she was switched to the extended trans-Pacific service. Four years later she opened a new route from Australia to Yokohama via Hong Kong. Later still, after three years spent predominantly cruising, the *Chusan* was sold in July 1973 for breaking up at Kaohsiung. The view (*previous page*) shows the *Chusan* berthed at Southampton on 17 August 1968. In the view (*above*), taken in April 1971, the *Chusan* sails from Cape Town while on a cruise. *John Edgington/Ian Shiffman*

Over her 25-year career, from February 1954, when she made her maiden voyage to Sydney from Tilbury, to February 1979, when she was paid off for breaking up in Taiwan, the *Arcadia* steamed 2,650,000 miles and carried more than 430,000 passengers. Ordered from John Brown & Company, Clydebank, the builders of the two Cunard 'Queens', the *Arcadia* was the first of two improved *Himalaya*-type ships. At 29,734 gross tons, she was somewhat larger than the earlier *Himalaya*, while her overall length of 721ft (219.8m) and beam of 90ft (27.4m) also exceeded the measurements of the earlier ship. Like her sister-ship *Iberia*, and the *Himalaya*, the *Arcadia* had a large cargo capacity, in the region of 260,000cu ft of general cargo and 235,000cu ft of refrigerated cargo. From the outset, the *Arcadia* cruised from Southampton each summer and spent the winter seasons on the scheduled service run to Australia. In her day she became one of the largest passenger ships to cruise Alaskan waters and was also the first P&O ship to visit Seattle. To mark the occasion, the city celebrated 'Arcadia Day' each 12 October. Prior to her disposal, from 1976 to the end of her career, the *Arcadia*'s cruise itinerary was focused on Australasia. This view shows the *Arcadia* departing Durban in May 1976.
Ian Shiffman

Above: The *Arcadia* photographed berthed at Southampton Docks in the early 1970s. *David Reed*

Right: Seen in a dawn arrival at Cape Town, the *Arcadia's* younger sister, the *Iberia*, built by Harland & Wolff at Belfast, enjoyed a comparatively brief career of just 18 years. Virtually identical in appearance and of approximately the same tonnage and dimensions, the *Iberia* could be distinguished from the *Arcadia* by the absence of a black top to her single funnel. She also had a distinctive cowl-type attachment to the top of her funnel which the *Arcadia* did not have. Like the

Arcadia, the *Iberia's* accommodation was for 675 First Class and 735 Tourist Class passengers. Although she commenced her maiden voyage from London, in September 1954, the *Iberia* was based at Southampton for much of her life, for both line voyages and cruises. In 1960, she and the *Arcadia* had air-conditioning installed throughout. Nine years later, in August 1969, the *Iberia* became the first liner to berth at Southampton's new Queen Elizabeth II passenger terminal, opened the previous month by HM The Queen and intended primarily for the new Cunarder *Queen Elizabeth 2*. For no apparent reason, it was the *Iberia* that was selected for

premature disposal, before even the older *Himalaya*, when the problems affecting the shipping industry in the early 1970s really began to bite. It was widely recognised that, with the move to permanent cruising and the emergence of purpose-built cruise ships, all combined passenger-cargo liners, designed for route service work, were under threat. But why the *Iberia* should have become such an unlucky early victim of these industry pressures is not known. It can only be concluded that she was either less popular or a less efficient vessel to operate. She was broken up at Kaohsiung, Taiwan, from September 1972. *Ian Shiffman*

After some six years working the Australia and trans-Pacific routes collaboratively, maintaining a twice-monthly service from the United Kingdom, P&O and Orient finally merged fully in May 1960, the result being that some six Orient ships took on a P&O identity of sorts from that date. Four of them subsequently became fully fledged units of the P&O fleet, registered with the company and painted in white and yellow livery. The old *Orion* was the exception, along with the even older *Orontes*. The black-hulled *Orontes*, soon laid up, was scrapped at Valencia, Spain, from March 1962. The *Orion*, which had pioneered the adoption of Orient Line's 'biscuit' or 'corn'-coloured hull livery, survived for another year, retaining her Orient Line paint scheme to the end, as shown here. One of a pair introduced before World War 2 — her sister *Orcades* was a war casualty, torpedoed on 10 October 1942 — the *Orion* was a radical ship, very much a trend-setter of her time. She was the first British liner to have an air-conditioning plant installed to improve passenger comfort in the tropics. Indeed, this was also the purpose of her new colours, as it was too for P&O's adoption of white paint on ship's hulls: to reduce the heat penetrating the hull plates. Furthermore, she had an open-air swimming pool in the space left by the omission of a mainmast. The *Orion* was also the first British ship to have a sprinkler-type fire protection system. Lavishly and stylishly appointed, she was an instant favourite on the Australia route, ranking in popularity with P&O's 'Straths' and the *Viceroy of India* (on the India run), all these vessels being commissioned during the same period. Wartime service interrupted her career, during which, after being requisitioned for conversion into a troopship, she acted as commodore ship for troop convoys. The *Orion* was, in April 1946, the first ship of either Orient or P&O to be handed back to her owners after the end of hostilities. She was reconditioned by her builders, Vickers Armstrong, resuming scheduled sailings in the Australia service from 25 February 1947. Seven years later, she was placed on the trans-Pacific service linking Sydney, Auckland, San Francisco and Vancouver. The *Orion* was broken up in Belgium from November 1963, after spending five months as a stationary hotel ship in Hamburg harbour. Over the course of her 28-year career she had steamed more than 2 million miles and carried ½ million passengers. Her gross tonnage was 23,371 and her dimensions were 665ft (202.7m) length overall and 82ft (25.0m) beam. She is pictured in the London docks, a photograph taken on 14 October 1956.
Ian Shiffman

The 1948-built Orient liner *Orcades* commemorated the sister-liner of the *Orion*, delivered in 1938 but lost during World War 2. Like all Orient Line ships completed postwar, the *Orcades* was built by Vickers Armstrong, Barrow. Electric arc welding was used extensively in her construction. In the design of the *Orcades*, the tradition of Orient Line layout was dramatically broken. Uncharacteristically, her bridge, mast and funnel were grouped together in a single, high structure placed amidships, resulting in the bridge being positioned much further aft than usual. This style was retained for the follow-on *Oronsay* and *Orsova*, which were introduced over the next six years. The *Orcades* was the first 'four-week' ship on the Australia run, permitting her to complete the passage from London to Sydney in 28 days at 22.5 knots average speed. She was also the first British ship to make a postwar cruise to the Mediterranean, in the summer of 1950.

Of similar proportions to the *Himalaya*, the *Orcades* had a gross tonnage of 28,396 and measured 711ft (216.7m) length overall and 90ft (27.4m) across her beam. Towards the end of her career, after the *Orcades* had joined P&O, she spent an increasing amount of time cruising. Her last voyage ended in October 1972. She was then broken up in Taiwan. The *Orcades* is shown here in the white and yellow colours of P&O that she adopted in 1964.
Ian Shiffman

Above: Second of Orient Line's new, postwar front-line ships was the *Oronsay*, seen here at Southampton in June 1963 in her original colours. Taking her name from another wartime casualty, the new *Oronsay* entered service on 10 May 1951 on the England to Australia run via Suez. She was marginally smaller than the earlier *Orcades*, but with the same steam turbine main propulsion system driving twin screws, she was also capable of a service speed of 22.5 knots. In 1954 the *Oronsay* inaugurated the extended trans-Pacific route, of what was later (from 1958) called Orient-Pacific Line, continuing to San Francisco and Vancouver before returning to London. She established a postwar record for the run from Sydney to Brisbane, completing the 515 miles distance in 24 hours. The *Oronsay*, along with the *Orcades* and later *Orsova*, had a narrow black stovepipe fitted to the top of her funnel to control smoke emissions. These appendages were soon popularly known as 'Welsh Hats'. Note the green boot-topping of the Orient colour scheme. The *Oronsay*, *Orcades*, *Orsova* and *Oriana* retained this colour for some years after adopting P&O white hulls, although they eventually switched to red boot-topping in keeping with P&O fashion. *Ray Sprake*

Right: The *Oronsay* is seen wearing P&O tropical livery. Scheduled to be paid off for disposal in 1972, the *Oronsay* was given a three-year reprieve. She finally went to the breakers in Taiwan in October 1975. *Don Smith*

In keeping with the Orient Line practice of pioneering novel features on its ships, the *Orsova*, completed in March 1954 and the largest of Orient's postwar trio, was the first ocean liner to dispense completely with a traditional mast. She was also the first large passenger ship to have an entirely welded hull. Comparable to P&O's *Arcadia* and *Iberia*, with which she was contemporary, the 28,790-gross-ton *Orsova* had an overall length of 723ft (220.4m) and a beam of 90ft (27.4m). She carried a total of 1,480 passengers in two classes. In April 1964, the *Orsova* marked the 50th anniversary of a unique event linking schools in the Commonwealth when she repeated the exchange of flags between Harbord Public School, Sydney, and All Saints Primary School, Freshwater, Isle of Wight. The flags of the original exchange had been conveyed in April 1914 aboard the *Orsova's* namesake, a vessel built in 1909 by John Brown & Company, Clydebank. *Ian Shiffman*

P&O retired the old *Corfu* and *Carthage* in 1961, at the end of 30-year-long careers that had covered both peacetime and wartime. To replace them, the company acquired the Compagnie Maritime Belge's five-year-old sister-ships *Jadotville* and *Baudouinville*, renaming them respectively as the *Chitral* and *Cathay*, the latter pictured here at Hong Kong. Built by Cockerill-Ougrée, Hoboken, Belgium, the *Baudouinville* entered service on the Antwerp to Congo and Angola route in November 1957. The service was suspended three years later when Belgium withdrew from its African colonies, leaving the two vessels surplus to requirements. With a gross tonnage of 13,921 and dimensions of 559ft (170.4m) length overall and a 70ft (21.3m) beam, the *Baudouinville* and her sister had only First Class accommodation for a maximum of 300 passengers. *Ian Shiffman*

The *Chitral* was completed as the *Jadotville* by Chantiers de St Nazaire, Penhöet, entering service in July 1956. Under the P&O house flag, accommodation on the former Belgian sisters was reduced to just over 200 berths. They joined the *Canton* on the intermediate service to the Far East, extending the route to the Japanese ports of Yokohama and Kobe. The *Chitral* made her first sailing from London and Southampton in March 1961, followed a month later by the *Cathay*. They were the first P&O ships to have an alternating-current electrical system. Both vessels had geared turbines giving them a service speed of 15 knots. After a brief spell cruising, the sisters transferred to the Australia to Far East route in 1969/70. The *Chitral* was scrapped in 1975. The *Cathay* outlived her, sold in the next year to the Chinese Government for employment as the merchant marine officers' training ship *Kengshin*, later renamed *Shanghai*. This photograph shows the *Chitral* in September 1967 departing Southampton behind an Alexandra Towing tug. *John Edgington*

One of the most innovative passenger ships ever built, and one of the two largest liners ever to be placed on the Australian express service via Suez, was the 41,930-gross-ton *Oriana*. Launched by Princess Alexandra at the Vickers Armstrong shipyard at Barrow on 3 November 1959 as an Orient Line ship, she commenced her maiden voyage from Southampton on 3 December 1960. She was spectacular, a one-off, much faster than any previous ship on the run. Equipped with geared turbines driving twin screws, she achieved a maximum speed of 30.64 knots during her trials, as fast as the two Cunard 'Queens'. The *Oriana* was designed to carry 2,100 passengers in accommodation that was splendid throughout, spread over 11 decks. She was the first large passenger ship to have bow and stern thrusters installed, and the first British liner to have a bulbous bow. She had fin stabilisers and carried a TV installation that permitted programme reception around the world, another first! Her small aft funnel is a dummy, concealing an engine-room ventilator shaft. The *Oriana* was registered as a P&O Steam Navigation ship in 1965, serving as a consort to the *Canberra*. After the collapse of the scheduled service to Australia in the early 1970s, she became a permanent cruise ship, working in the northern hemisphere in summer and the southern in winter. She sailed around the world in 1971, a voyage-cum-cruise that lasted 66 days with calls at 19 ports. In November 1981 the *Oriana* was transferred to Sydney to launch a new career, cruising all year round in Australasian and South Pacific waters, which ended her long association with Southampton, her home port in the United Kingdom. P&O sold her to the Daiwa House Group, Japan, in May 1986 for conversion into a stationary tourist centre located in Beppu Bay, Kyushu. Still carrying her original name, the *Oriana* is now moored at Shanghai, providing, amongst other things, a club environment for ex-patriot Westerners living in the Chinese city. *Ian Shiffman*

Probably P&O's most famous ship, the Harland & Wolff-built *Canberra* was described as 'the ship of the century' when she entered service on 2 June 1961. She was the largest British-built liner since the *Queen Elizabeth* of 1940. Bigger than the *Oriana*, at 45,733 gross tons, the *Canberra* was also longer, at 820ft (249.9m), and beamier, at 102ft (31.1m). Like the *Oriana*, the *Canberra* was a unique ship featuring distinctive engines-aft styling. Taking advantage of the uncluttered space in the centre of the ship, her public rooms, as well as the vast open spaces of her upper deck, were unsurpassed. In the *Canberra*, P&O went back to a turbo-electric propulsion installation, the first since the 1930s. Producing 88,000 shaft horsepower, it gave her a maximum speed of 29.27 knots. Between them, the *Canberra* and *Oriana* reduced the passage time from the UK to Australia from four to three weeks, at a service speed of 27.5 knots, the fastest times ever achieved on the routes 'down under'. The *Canberra* made a successful transition to full-time, all-year-round cruising after the scheduled service trade to Australia dried up. A feature of her annual cruise programme was a three/four-month world cruise. Here she arrives at Tenerife, Canary Islands, during one of her shorter cruises from Southampton.
Ian Shiffman

The *Canberra* is seen at Southampton, alongside Berths 39 and 40, with the new *Oriana* beyond her in the Ocean Dock. Symbolic of her eclipse, the retiring *Canberra* is in shadow while the new addition to the P&O fleet stands out in bright sunshine.
David Reed

Left and above: P&O's first involvement in short-sea scheduled ferry services, through its subsidiary General Steam Navigation, was with North Sea Ferries, sailing between Hull and Rotterdam from 1965, and with Normandy Ferries, on the cross-Channel routes from 1967. Through a process of change of partners and progressive acquisitions, the South Coast operation was redesignated as part of P&O Ferries and the ships adopted the company houseflag symbol on their funnels and the legend 'P&O Ferries' painted in white letters on the sides of their pale blue hulls. At the time, P&O boasted that it was the only company to include a reclining sleeper-seat and rug in the ticket price for crossings on its vessels. How things have moved on since then!

The *Dragon*, shown here, was one of the first two vessels to be employed on the services from Southampton, and later Portsmouth, to Le Havre. Her sister was the *Leopard*. Other vessels in the P&O Ferries fleet at that time were the *Lion*, *Panther* and *Tiger*. For a brief period, the company also operated a pair of Boeing Jetfoils on a fast route between St Katharine's Dock, London, and Zeebrugge. Built in 1967 by Dubigeon-Normandie SA and Ateliers et Chantiers de Bretagne, at Nantes, the *Dragon* was registered with the General Steam Navigation Company. The almost identical *Leopard* was owned by S.A.G.A. until 1976. The *Dragon's* gross tonnage was 6,141 and she measured 442ft (134.7m) length and 72ft (21.9m) beam. Both ships could

accommodate 850 passengers and had capacity for 250 cars and 45 lorries. At the beginning of 1985, just 10 years after the formation of P&O Ferries, the group sold off its entire cross-Channel operation, which was making substantial and steady losses, to European Ferries plc. The concern also took the *Leopard*. The *Dragon* was transferred instead to the Felixstowe-based P&O European Ferries and was renamed *Ionic Ferry*. Subsequently, she and her sister were sold on to new owners, working for periods in the waters of the Mediterranean, the Black Sea and the Caribbean. In the view (*left*) the *Dragon* wears Normandy Ferries colours. The view (*above*) shows her as a P&O Ferries ship. *Ian Shiffman/David Reed*

Left: The early 1970s marked a turning point in P&O's ocean passenger business, ending one phase and opening another that proved to be equally prosperous. From that time, all new ships commissioned by the company were purpose-built for luxury cruising whereas all the older vessels had to be adapted for the purpose, many of them not totally suiting this transition. P&O's first dedicated cruise ship was the *Spirit of London*, seen (*left*) arriving at San Francisco. She was a small ship at 17,370 gross tons, built by Cantieri Navali del Tirreno e Riuniti at Riva Trigoso, Italy. In fact, she was purchased on the slipway, having been ordered by Klosters Rederi A/S, Oslo. Cruising under the P&O banner, the *Spirit of London* made her maiden sailing from Southampton on 11 November 1972, bound for San Juan, from where she maintained an itinerary of cruises on the US west coast. A diesel ship, the *Spirit of London* was 536ft (163.4m) long and 75ft (22.9m) wide. She carried 700 passengers in a single category, all with the full run of the ship. Only the fare categories distinguished the grade and location of the accommodation — internal or external, suite with day rooms or small two-, three- or four-berth cabin. *Ian Shiffman*

Right: The *Spirit of London* is seen from the stern, high and dry in dry dock. *Ian Shiffman*

Below: Princess Cruises Inc of Seattle had been established in 1964 by the industrialist Stan McDonald, initially operating converted British Columbia ferries on excursions to Alaska and, later, Mexico. The company soon flourished as its novel cruise programme proved particularly appealing to the US market, especially to younger passengers. P&O acquired Princess Cruises in August 1974 as part of its expanding involvement in shipping tourism and to give it a vital stake in the lucrative North American cruise market. Around the same time, two larger purpose-built cruise ships were purchased to increase the number of available passenger berths,

in response to the growing level of demand in this sector. Ordered originally for the Norwegian Cruise Ships A/S consortium (Lorentzen A/S and Fearnley & Eger), they were the *Sea Venture* and *Island Venture*. Both vessels measured approximately 20,000 gross tons and accommodated 767 passengers. They were built in the Emden yard of Rheinstahl Nordseewerke GmbH. Fitted with geared diesels driving twin screws, they had a speed of 21.5 knots. Their main dimensions were 553ft (168.6m) overall length and 81ft (24.7m) beam. After crossing the Atlantic from Oslo, they inaugurated a New York to Bermuda service, reminiscent of the

'Millionaires' cruises of Furness Bermuda Line in the 1930s and 1950s. The *Island Venture* had already been renamed *Island Princess* in 1972 by Flagship Cruises, pre-empting the identity that would befit her status as a unit of the burgeoning Princess Cruises fleet, and the *Sea Venture* was renamed *Pacific Princess* by P&O in 1975. For their employment on the US West Coast circuit, P&O had the accommodation aboard the *Pacific Princess* and *Island Princess* (pictured here) modified, lowering their maximum passenger capacity to 646 berths on each ship. P&O was fortunate to have the *Island Princess* and *Pacific Princess* selected for the shooting of

the popular television programme *The Love Boat*. Transmitted to millions of American viewers, the series was conceived to promote the image of cruising as an activity as much for the pleasure of the young, lively and adventurous as it was for the old and well-heeled. There is no doubt that *The Love Boat* was a primary catalyst for the rapid growth of the North American cruise industry in the 1970s, much to the benefit of P&O. Withdrawn in 2000, the *Island Princess* was sold to Hyundai Cruises and renamed *Hyundai Pungak*, but since Hyundai's collapse she has sailed under the name *Platinum*. *Bettina Rohbrecht*

Below: Following the acquisition by P&O of Princess Cruises, the *Spirit of London* was transferred to the US subsidiary in October 1974 and renamed *Sun Princess*. As the *Sun Princess* she spent 14 years cruising for the American market, based on the West Coast. This picture shows her at Vancouver on 2 October 1982. However, as the cruise holiday business expanded and the need emerged for larger ships with more passenger berths, the *Sun Princess* became inadequate for the scale

of the Princess Cruises operation. She was sold to Premier Cruise Line in September 1988 and renamed *Majestic*. After a comprehensive refit at Bremerhaven by Lloyd Werft, she was restyled as the *Starship Majestic* from May 1989 and based at Port Canaveral, making cruises to the Bahamas. The former *Spirit of London* now sails as the *Flamenco*, registered under the ownership of Festival Cruises. *Ian Shiffman*

Left and above: The Princess Cruises fleet benefited from a significant enhancement in January 1979, in the form of the *Sea Princess*, larger than and superior to all its existing vessels. Purchased the previous year, she was the former *Kungsholm*, the last and finest of the ships built to serve under the flag of the 'Tre Kronor', the house flag of the Swedish America Line. Built by John Brown & Co, Clydebank, she was launched on 14 April 1965 and made her maiden voyage from Gothenburg to New York on 22 April 1966. The *Kungsholm* was one of relatively few transatlantic scheduled service passenger liners to have diesel propulsion. In the event, she made very few line voyages, switching to full-time cruising almost immediately. With the termination of all Swedish America passenger services, the *Kungsholm* was sold in August 1975 to Flagship Cruises, Monrovia, for whom she made cruises from New York under her original name. After P&O acquired her, she was reconstructed by Bremer Vulkan at Vegesack, with both interiors and exterior being dramatically remodelled. The most noticeable change to her appearance was the removal of her forward funnel along with the heightening of the stern-most funnel, which remained. Her gross tonnage was raised to 27,670 but her hull dimensions of 660ft (201.2m) length and 87ft (26.5m) beam were left unaltered. For the first three years of her P&O career, spent cruising in Far East and Australian waters as well as on the American West Coast, the *Sea Princess* wore the colours of Princess Cruises, as shown in the photograph (*left*) of her at Vancouver. However, from 1982 the *Sea Princess* transferred to the UK, making European cruises from Southampton, repainted in P&O Cruises livery. These views on this page show her berthed at the Queen Elizabeth II Terminal, Southampton, in August 1982.
Bettina Rohbrecht / David L. Williams (x2)

The cruising phase of the *Canberra's* career was abruptly interrupted when the British Government took her over for trooping to the Falkland Islands in the spring of 1982. Dubbed the 'Great White Whale', she sailed from Southampton as part of the South Atlantic Task Force on 9 April 1982, returning dirty and untidy but triumphant on 11 July of the same year. Here she is seen arriving at her home port, surrounded by welcoming small craft. The *Canberra* resumed cruising at the end of that August, after a thorough refit, more popular than ever. At the end of a long, varied and highly successful career, she was finally sold for breaking up in October 1997, her last voyage taking her to the breaker's yard at Gadani Beach, Pakistan. Despite her popularity, to raise her to the latest SOLAS cruise ship safety standards would have proved too expensive. *Ian Shiffman*

As a striking demonstration of P&O's intentions to commission equally grand and capacious cruise ships for both its UK- and USA-based cruise operations — the latter being Princess Cruises — the *Royal Princess* was introduced to the US market in November 1984. Prior to her positioning voyage from Southampton, she was officially christened in a ceremony performed by HRH the Princess of Wales. For this splendid, decoratively stunning vessel, then one of the largest dedicated cruise ships in the world, P&O placed the construction order with the Finnish shipyard, O/Y Wärtsilä A/B, Helsinki. Remaining as an active vessel in the present Princess Cruises fleet, the 44,348-gross-ton *Royal Princess* has an overall length of 757ft (230.7m) and a beam of 96ft (29.3m). She accommodates 1,260 passengers. Geared diesels driving twin screws give her a speed of 22 knots. The *Royal Princess* typifies the design of the modern cruise ship, which began to enter service from the early 1980s, in having her lifeboats stowed low down to leave a greater area of uncluttered recreation space on the upper decks. Likewise, her passenger staterooms are located in the upper decks whereas her restaurants, lounges and theatre have been deliberately placed on the lower decks. *Ian Shiffman*

Below: The *Royal Princess* is seen here from the stern quarter, making her way along Southampton Water, inward bound for the docks at the time of her inaugural visit. *David Reed*

Right: A year after disposing of its original cross-Channel services, P&O acquired a controlling interest in a company which held more than 20% of the share equity of the European Ferries Group plc. Later that same year, a favourable judgement from the Monopolies & Mergers Commission cleared the way for P&O to bid for the balance of the voting shares in the company, which it did. P&O was once more in the cross-Channel ferry business! The acquisition included the extensive route network and fleet of ships owned by Townsend Thoresen, operating across the English Channel and southern North Sea. Just two months after the takeover, one of these vessels, the *Herald of Free Enterprise*, capsized off Zeebrugge in an accident which cost 193 lives. Apart from the implementation of safety modifications and the tightening up of shipboard procedures, the sinking also precipitated a fleetwide renaming exercise that eliminated the words 'Free Enterprise' from all the ships' names. Among the vessels affected was the *Spirit of Free Enterprise* which became the *Pride of Kent*. Completed in January 1980 by the Schichau Unterweser AG shipyard, Bremerhaven, she measured 7,951 gross tons with an overall length of 433ft (132.0m). In 1991 she was taken in hand for lengthening and widening by Fincantieri Navali Italiani SpA, Palermo, as a result of which her gross tonnage increased to 20,446. Her revised dimensions were 536ft (163.4m) length and 86ft (26.2m) beam. The *Pride of Kent's* capacity was for 1,825 deck passengers, 461 private cars and 64 trucks. This view of her was taken in May 1997. *Ian Shiffman*

Below: Four of the older vessels in the Townsend Thoresen fleet taken over by P&O were the *Viking Valiant*, *Viking Venturer*, *Viking Viscount* and *Viking Voyager*, all built by Aalborg Vaerft A/S, Aalborg, Denmark. They entered service on the cross-Channel routes from Southampton, later Portsmouth, between January 1975 and May 1976. The quartet retained their original names for some two years after joining P&O. As built, they measured approximately 6,400 gross tons with an overall length of 422ft (128.6m) and a beam of 65ft (19.8m). Passenger capacity was for 1,327, of whom 282 could be accommodated in cabin berths. Two of the four ships, the *Viking Venturer* and *Viking Valiant*, were jumboised by the Schichau Unterweser AG shipyard over the period from December 1985 to June 1986. The enlargement process gave the pair a new tonnage measurement of 14,760 gross and their dimensions increased to 471ft (143.6m) overall length and 72ft (21.9m) beam. Interestingly, passenger numbers barely changed, the extra capacity being devoted to greater deck space for private cars, the number of which increased from 275 to 370, or commercial vehicles. Here the *Viking Venturer* is seen painted in the attractive dark blue livery which was introduced in 1987 to coincide with the renaming of the ferries business as P&O European Ferries Ltd. *Bettina Rohbrecht*

In July 1989 the four vessels of the *Viking Venturer* series were renamed to fit in with the modern, corporate image that P&O had adopted to help promote its ferry business in a positive, confident and appealing fashion. Thereafter, all P&O ferries had names prefixed by the word 'Pride'. This is the *Pride of Cherbourg*, formerly the *Viking Voyager*, one of the two non-jumboised ships. The other was the *Pride of Winchester*, ex-*Viking Viscount*. *Ian Shiffman*

The *Viking Venturer* became the *Pride of Hampshire*. From 1990, with the splitting of the P&O European Ferries operations into regional divisions, the *Pride of Hampshire* was reregistered under the ownership of P&O European Ferries (Portsmouth) Ltd. Her partner, the other stretched ferry, was the *Pride of Le Havre*, ex-*Viking Valiant*.
Ian Shiffman

The standard of ferry commissioned for the Hull to Rotterdam route of North Sea Ferries, of which P&O was a partner until 1996, had also been steadily improving, culminating in two particularly well-appointed vessels placed on the service in 1987. They were the *Norsea*, registered with P&O Steam Navigation Company, and the *Norsun*, owned by Hollandsche Vrachtvaart Maatshappij BV (Royal Nedlloyd). The *Norsea* was the last P&O ship to be constructed by a British shipyard. Built by Govan Shipbuilders, Glasgow, she was launched by HM Queen Elizabeth, The Queen Mother on 9 September 1986. Construction of the *Norsun* was entrusted to Nippon Kokan KK at its Tsurumi shipyard, Yokohama. The *Norsea* has a gross tonnage of 31,785 and her principal dimensions are 589ft (179.5m) length and 82ft (25.0m) beam. She entered service in May 1987, raising the traffic capacity on the North Sea crossing with her accommodation for 764 berthed passengers (in 446 cabins) and 504 deck passengers. Vehicle deck space provides for 850 private cars or 180 12m-long trailer units or a mix of the two. Although she was a P&O ship, the *Norsea* retained the distinctive North Sea Ferries colour scheme until 1996 when the P&O dark blue livery was adopted by what had, by then, become P&O North Sea Ferries. *Govan Shipbuilders*

Sister to the *Norsea*, the Japanese-built *Norsun* became a wholly owned P&O ship in 1996 when Royal Nedlloyd agreed to the sale of its 50% stake in North Sea Ferries to the P&O Steam Navigation Company. She was also repainted in P&O colours. With a gross tonnage of 31,598, the *Norsun* has broadly similar dimensions and carrying capacity to the *Norsea*. The *Norsea* and *Norsun* have recently undergone a major refurbishment to coincide with the introduction of two new cruise ferries, as they have been called, on the Hull to Rotterdam route. The work involved increasing the cabin accommodation and improving the restaurant facilities, in preparation for their transfer to the Hull to Zeebrugge route. *Ian Shiffman*

Above: P&O's major fleet enhancement programme, embarked upon from the mid-1980s, expanded and upgraded all sectors of its passenger shipping business. This benefited the ferry operators across the North Sea and English Channel as much as it did the cruise fleets of P&O Cruises (as it had been styled) and Princess Cruises. Simultaneous with the *Norsea* and *Norsun* on the North Sea crossing, two jumbo ferries ordered by Townsend Thoresen, then the largest on the Dover to Calais route, were taken over on the stocks at Schichau Unterweser AG, Bremen Vegesack. Named *Pride of Dover* and *Pride of Calais*, they have a tonnage of 26,433 gross and dimensions of 558ft (170.1m) length and 91ft (27.7m) beam. This is the *Pride of Dover*, which entered service in May 1987.
Bettina Rohbrecht

Right: Sister-ferry, the *Pride of Calais*, commenced cross-Channel sailings in November 1987. The *Pride of Dover* and *Pride of Calais* can accommodate 90 berthed passengers in twin cabins and 2,260 deck passengers. Of ro-ro design, their vehicle capacity is for either 650 private cars or 104 lorries, or a mix of the two. They are operated by P&O European Ferries (Dover) Ltd. *Bettina Rohbrecht*

P&O celebrated its 150th birthday in July 1987 with the *Pacific Princess* as the focal point. She sailed up the River Thames to Greenwich, London, specially for the occasion, decked out with bunting and floodlit at night. On the evening of 7 July the anniversary culminated in a royal banquet aboard the ship and a huge fireworks display. It was altogether a more exuberant affair than the centenary celebrations of 50 years earlier . Since then, after a career cruising to many parts of the world, the *Pacific Princess* has been sold to an Italian concern which will also take her fleet-mate *Victoria*, ex-*Sea Princess*, when both become available late in 2002.
P&O

In September 1988 Sitmar Cruises of Monrovia was taken over by P&O. With the acquisition came three older converted ships, a sizeable modern four-year-old cruise ship and three much larger vessels either under construction or on order. Two of the old ships were former Cunard liners, originally built in the 1950s for the service from Liverpool to Montreal. Products of the Clydebank yard of John Brown & Company, they had entered service as the *Carinthia* and *Sylvania* in June 1956 and June 1957 respectively. After a brief spell cruising for Cunard, they were sold in January 1968 to the Vlasov Group (Sitmar Line) for a proposed service from Southampton to New Zealand via Italy and Greece. When this fell through, they languished for almost two years until they underwent a comprehensive reconstruction at Trieste. Already renamed the *Fairland*, the former *Carinthia* re-emerged in 1971 as the cruise ship *Fairsea*. She spent the next 17 years cruising for Sitmar from US ports. Following her transfer to P&O in September 1988, she was renamed *Fair Princess*, her cruising career in the US market continuing until February 1997, when she was relocated first at Sydney and then at Auckland. Since leaving the P&O fleet in June 2000 she has had varied but faltering employment. Apparently renamed *Emerald Fortune* for gambling trips from Hong Kong, it was reported that she had been chartered instead to the Hainan local government to promote cruises for the Chinese domestic market under the name *China Seas Discovery*.
Ian Shiffman

The career of the *Dawn Princess* has followed along similar lines to that of the *Fair Princess*. After 20 years in the ownership of Sitmar Line as the *Fairwind*, she was selected to introduce Sitmar's new house colours in 1988 when she was simultaneously renamed *Sitmar Fairwind*. In the event, she was the only vessel to make the transition, a short-lived experiment which ended with her sale to P&O the same year. Measuring 21,989 gross tons when delivered to Cunard in 1957, the major interior modifications carried out in 1970/1 had raised her tonnage. By 1990, after further alterations, it measured 24,803 gross tons. Her dimensions, the same as those of the *Fair Princess*, were 608ft (185.3m) length overall and 80ft (24.4m) beam. Reflecting their greater vintage, they were steam turbine-powered ships. No longer with P&O, replaced by a larger purpose-built cruise vessel, the *Dawn Princess* returned to the Vlasov Group in 1993, since when she has sailed for the Silver Line as the *Albatros*. This view shows her prior to leaving P&O, at Vancouver on 21 July 1990. *Ian Shiffman*

Sitmar Cruises' only new cruise ship at the time of the 1988 takeover was the 46,392-gross-ton *Fairsky*, a steam turbine-powered vessel — the only modern cruise ship to have this engine system — completed by the Chantiers du Nord et de la Méditerranée shipyard, La Seyne, in April 1984. Her length measurement is 789ft (240.5m) and she is 91ft (27.7m) across the beam. Transferred to Princess Cruises and renamed *Sky Princess*, she worked cruise itineraries for the US market until November 1999 when she was repositioned at Sydney for Australian cruise service, displacing the *Fair Princess*, which was moved to Auckland, New Zealand. The *Sky Princess* became the *Pacific Sky*, serving P&O Holidays, a new cruise operating company created for the Australasian market. As such, she has been unique in the present-day P&O Group passenger fleet in having a name which does not fit in with any P&O naming convention, either current or historic. This photograph shows the *Sky Princess* at Vancouver on 29 July 1994. *Ian Shiffman*

Left: Nearing completion at the time of P&O's takeover of Sitmar was the *Sitmar Fair Majesty*, a 63,524-gross-ton cruise ship, launched under her planned name at the Chantiers de L'Atlantique shipyard, St Nazaire, on 5 March 1988. She entered service in March 1989 under the new name *Star Princess*, following the official naming ceremony at Florida. A considerable improvement on the *Fairsky*, grander and larger in all respects, measuring 810ft (246.9m) in length and 106ft (32.3m) beam, the *Star Princess* was also, as a further contrast, a diesel-engined ship. She could accommodate 1,621 passengers in a single class. In another photograph taken at Vancouver, the *Star Princess* is seen on 16 July 1999. *Ian Shiffman*

Above: Berthed in the Ocean Dock at Southampton, this view of *Star Princess* was taken early in the morning, shortly after her arrival. *David Reed*

The first of the two even larger cruise ships ordered by Sitmar, prior to its acquisition, from the Fincantieri Navali Italiani SpA shipyard, Monfalcone, was destined to enter service as the *Crown Princess*. She made her maiden cruise in July 1990. Having an ultra-modern enclosed profile, albeit topped by a single conventional funnel, the *Crown Princess* has a maximum passenger capacity of 1,990, almost the same as the old *Fairstar*, ex-*Oxfordshire*, a ship of less than one third her size. Along with the extra space, her décor and extensive passenger amenities reflected the standard that Princess Cruises was offering passengers on its front-line ships, targeted at the competitive American market. At 69,845 gross tons, the *Crown Princess* and her sister, *Regal Princess*, measures 811ft (247.2m) overall length and 106ft (13.3m) beam, dimensions that still permit them to navigate the Panama Canal. *Ian Shiffman*

The *Golden Princess*, first of the name, was built as the *Royal Viking Sky* for Royal Viking Line in June 1973. Built by O/Y Wärtsilä A/B, Helsinki, as the second of a trio of identical cruise ships, she measured 21,891 gross tons and had dimensions of 583ft (177.7m) length and 83ft (25.3m) beam, as completed. Nine years after entering service, in September 1982, the *Royal Viking Sky* arrived at the AG Weser Seebeckwerft yard at Bremerhaven to be stretched, by the insertion of an additional midships hull section. She emerged from the reconstruction a much sleeker vessel, her overall length increased to 674ft (205.4m) giving her a revised tonnage of 28,078 gross. She was renamed *Sunward* in 1991, four years after transferring to Norwegian Caribbean Lines, only to be renamed again in the same year when she was sold to Birka Line. As the *Birka Queen*, she was employed making short cruises to Latvia and Russia from Stockholm. Barely a year later she was chartered back to Norwegian Caribbean Lines, assuming the name *Sunward* for a second time. Subsequently, P&O took the ship from Birka Line in a three-year charter to replace the *Dawn Princess* for cruises to Hawaii, Tahiti, the South Pacific islands and the Far East. She was once more renamed, becoming the *Golden Princess*. At the end of the charter period, in 1998, Birka Line sold her to Star Cruises which gave her the name *Superstar Capricorn*, her sixth identity. She has since been renamed yet again, as the *Hyundai Keumgang*, under charter to Hyundai Cruises, Korea. *Bettina Rohbrecht*

Above: Emanating from the same shipyard as her sister, the *Pride of Portsmouth*, this is the *Pride of Le Havre*, ex-*Olau Hollandia*, built in 1989. The port facilities at both Portsmouth and Le Havre are, apparently, about to undergo major redevelopment and improvement, part of an overall programme to upgrade the cross-Channel services on the central routes to the Continent. It has been intimated that, as part of this process, P&O

may commission new ships to replace these chartered ro-ro ferries. *Ian Shiffman*

Right: Another view of the cross-Channel ferry *Pride of Portsmouth*. Competition on the routes to France from Portsmouth has intensified over recent years, with the P&O ships vying for business with the large ferries introduced by Brittany Ferries on the run to Caen and St Malo. Excellent motorway links

to Paris from both Caen and Le Havre, P&O's port, have neutralised any such advantage one route may have had over the other. Thus, the selection of cross-Channel passage is now largely dependent on fare price, shipboard facilities and quality of service, all areas where P&O hopes to succeed over its rival. *P&O European Ferries*

The P&O European Ferries (Portsmouth) operation was extended in 1993 by the addition of a service across the Bay of Biscay to Bilbao and Santander in northern Spain, resurrecting a service briefly run in the early 1970s with another part-owned P&O ferry, the *Eagle*. To maintain the present programme of sailings, P&O acquired the former Baltic ferry *Olympia* from Viking Line and renamed her *Pride of Bilbao*. At the time she was the largest short-sea ferry in service with any British operator. Completed in April 1986 for her original owners by O/Y Wärtsilä A/B, Åbo, the *Pride of Bilbao* has a gross tonnage of 37,799 and is able to accommodate 2,545 passengers — 2,333 in berths — with capacity for 600 private cars. Her main dimensions are 590ft (179.8m) length overall and 93ft (28.3m) beam. She can be regarded as the very first P&O 'cruise ferry'. Befitting the demands of her longer 72-hour passages to and from Spain, the *Pride of Bilbao* has extensive entertainment and recreational amenities for the enjoyment of her passengers. Designed originally for service on the route between Stockholm and Helsinki, she is well suited to the sea conditions off France's Atlantic coast. *Bettina Rohbrecht/Ian Shiffman*

Above: Having already spent some 13 years cruising from Southampton, the *Sea Princess* was absorbed fully into the UK-based P&O Cruises operation in 1995, restyled as the *Victoria*. This released her former name for adoption by the third of the four new cruise ships being constructed for Princess Cruises at Monfalcone. Despite her age and traditional layout, designed for a combination of scheduled service voyages and off-peak cruises, the *Victoria* remains an enduring favourite with a regular clientele. Sadly, her P&O days are numbered, for she is due for retirement in November 2002. *Bettina Rohrbrecht*

Right: Continuing expansion of the UK and European cruise market led P&O to order a large new cruise ship for this operation from the Meyer Werft shipyard, Papenburg, Germany, on which was bestowed the name of the last and greatest of the Orient Line ships. This gesture was warmly received by the shipping press and ocean liner buffs alike, signifying a perpetuation of the former Orient Line traditions within the modern P&O passenger fleet. Named by HM Queen Elizabeth II in May 1995, the second *Oriana*,

at 69,153 gross tons, was P&O's largest new passenger ship since the *Canberra* of 1961. Despite early teething problems with her propellers, she soon settled into a cruise itinerary working from Southampton. The *Oriana* measures 850ft (259.1m) length overall and 105ft (32.0m) across her beam. She is a most elegant ship, hinting at the old *Canberra* but with a distinctive modern look. A twin-screw vessel, driven by diesel engines, she has a service speed of 24 knots. *Bettina Rohrbrecht*

Above: The new *Oriana* is seen departing Cape Town on 21 January 2002. *Ian Shiffman*

Right: The old *Oriana*, no longer with P&O, is seen in May 2002 berthed in the River Huangpo at Pudong, on Shanghai's waterfront. The ship is currently undergoing an extensive refurbishment but her future role is not known. As part of the overhaul, flat-sided structures have been welded on both sides of her hull, both forward and aft, but their purpose is equally unknown. *David L. Williams*

Left: In recognition of the success of the *Crown Princess* and *Regal Princess*, P&O went back to Fincantieri for more, improved ships of this type, a second group which ultimately comprised four vessels. Somewhat larger at 77,500 gross tons, their dimensions are 857ft (261.2m) overall length and 106ft (32.3m) beam. The first to be delivered, in November 1995, was the *Sun Princess*, followed by the *Dawn Princess* in April 1997. Before even the second ship was completed, P&O ordered two more ships of the class, so popular had the *Sun Princess* already proved to be. The third ship, *Sea Princess*, was launched at Monfalcone on 23 January 1998 and delivered to Princess Cruises in October of that year. The *Sun Princess* is seen arriving at Vancouver. *Ian Shiffman*

Left: Last of the group, the *Ocean Princess* followed the *Sea Princess* into service in February 2000. More or less identical to her three earlier sisters, she was christened in New York by the film actors Ali McGraw and Ryan O'Neill. Based on the US West Coast and making cruises to Canada and Alaska, these four ships also spend time cruising in the Caribbean, their size being within the navigable limits of the Panama Canal. In part to replace the *Victoria* when she goes out of P&O service at the end of the 2002 season, the *Ocean Princess* will be switched to P&O Cruises, commencing with a Mexican cruise in November. She has been given the new name *Oceana*, another name with a long heritage with P&O, having been previously the identity of one of the four 'Jubilee' class ships of the late 19th century. The *Oceana* is scheduled to transfer her home port to Southampton, probably when the *Arcadia* leaves for the Mediterranean. In keeping with group colour schemes, the *Oceana's* funnel will lose the flowing locks of Princess Cruises' mermaid symbol, and will be painted instead in a coat of plain yellow. The *Ocean Princess* sails from Vancouver in this view. *Ian Shiffman*

To replace the *Canberra* when her career ended in 1997, P&O transferred the *Star Princess*, ex-*Sitmar Fair Majesty*, to Southampton to bolster the burgeoning UK cruise market. Following an overhaul at Harland & Wolff, Belfast, she commenced her new duties in November 1997 under the name *Arcadia*, reviving the memory of yet another popular former P&O passenger liner, retired some 18 years earlier. As it has turned out, the *Arcadia's* tour of duty at Southampton has proved to be short-lived, for she is now heading off to a Mediterranean base to commence a series of cruises catering specifically for younger passengers. under the suitably-styled, new 'Ocean Village' brand name. She will be replaced at Southampton by the *Sea Princess* which is to be re-christened *Adonia*. *Bettina Rohbrecht*

With the commissioning of the Fincantieri-built *Grand Princess* in 1998, P&O and Princess Cruises joined the 100,000-ton club, as the size of new cruise ships continued to soar. Briefly the largest passenger ship in the world, at 108,806 gross tons, her hull measurements are 951ft (289.9m) length and 118ft (36.0m) beam. She stands high above the water, too — at 201ft (61.3m) she is taller than both Nelson's Column and the Niagara Falls. After opening her inaugural season on 26 May 1988 with a voyage from Istanbul to Barcelona, the *Grand Princess* crossed the Atlantic at the end of that summer, arriving at New York on 29 September 1998 to a classic ticker-tape reception. As a major PR event, no ship could possibly have received a grander début on the US scene. With her moored off the Statue of Liberty, the visit culminated in the floodlighting of the Empire State Building in the P&O house flag colours, while the VIP guests and passengers were treated to a spectacular firework display over lower Manhattan. Her sister-ship, and second of the class, the *Golden Princess*, embarked upon her career three years later. Ordered in January 1998 and completed at the same Fincantieri shipyard, the *Golden Princess* entered service in April 2001 at the end of a week of mini-cruises organised exclusively for representatives of the European travel industry. She is seen in the Solent, sailing from Southampton, at the end of her only visit to the port, bound for her summer cruise base in the Mediterranean. The other view shows her berthed in one of the European ports she visited, prior to her departure for warmer climes. *David L. Williams*

In the face of competition from the newly opened Channel Tunnel and the Eurostar rail link, P&O entered into an operational agreement with Stena Line in March 1998 to operate their combined fleets on the short Dover to Calais crossing collaboratively. As a consequence, since then both companies' ferries working this route have adopted the P&O-Stena brand name on their sides, as shown here on the *Pride of Dover*. A red band has also been added to her hull and her funnel now carries the Stena Line house flag in addition to that of P&O. *Bettina Rohbrecht*

Above: Constructed by Schichau Seebeckwerft AG at Fischereihafen, Bremerhaven, to the account of P&O European Ferries (Dover), the *Pride of Burgundy* entered service in 1993. At 28,138 gross tons, she is one of the largest P&O passenger vessels now working on the crossing from Dover to Calais. She has accommodation for 194 berthed passengers and 1,447 deck passengers in addition to capacity for 600 private cars or an equivalent lane space of commercial vehicles. Her dimensions are 588ft (179.2m) length and 93ft (28.3m) beam. She is seen here after the formation of the co-operative partnership between P&O and Stena Line A/B of Sweden. *Bettina Rohbrecht*

Right: P&O's *Victoria* undertook a special charter cruise at the time of the millennium celebrations, to commemorate the Cape mail service operated from Southampton by the Union Castle Line from 1900 until 1977. For this celebratory cruise, her funnel was repainted in the colours of Union Castle. *Ian Shiffman*

Above: The continuing upsurge in cruising from the UK prompted P&O to add another large ship to the Southampton-based cruise fleet, an enlarged *Oriana*, ordered from the same builders, Meyer Werft, Papenburg. Her keel was laid on 15 December 1998 and she was floated out of her covered building dock on 3 February 1999. Christened at the Mayflower Terminal, Southampton, in April 2000 by HRH The Princess Royal, the *Aurora* is a stylish, elegant ship, combining grace with size. She measures 76,152 gross tons and is 886ft (270.1m) long, rather longer than the *Oriana* although they have the same beam dimension. The *Aurora* has staterooms for a maximum of 2,100 passengers, some 125 more than the *Oriana*. However, unlike the *Oriana*, her accommodation has been distributed in such a way that a higher percentage of passengers have private balconies or verandahs. The *Aurora* can be distinguished by the unique, concave elliptical transom stern, below her terraced aft decks. She is the first P&O Cruises ship to have diesel-electric propulsion, a development introduced into the Princess Cruises fleet with the *Sun Princess* of 1995. As a measure of P&O's confidence in the future prospects for the booming UK and European cruise market, an even larger, yet-to-be-named ship has been ordered from Fincantieri. The 109,000-gross-ton vessel, of the same class as the *Grand Princess*, may, however, not be built, in the wake of the terrorist attacks of 11 September 2001. Just prior to her speed trials, the *Aurora* is seen moored outside the Meyer Werft covered building yard on the River Ems at Papenburg. *Meyer Werft*

Right: In this second view of the vessel, the *Aurora* is captured in bright sunlight in the Solent as she makes a departure from Southampton. *David Reed*

Above: The *Aurora* is seen here at Cape Town during a call she made to the South African port on 13 March 2002. *Ian Shiffman*

Right: This photograph, showing the distinctive stern end of the *Aurora*, was taken while she was alongside at Southampton's Mayflower Terminal in June 2000. The aft decks terrace down above her inverted transom stern in which large, picture windows afford unspoilt views over the ocean for diners in her Alexandria Restaurant. *David L. Williams*

AURORA

LONDON

Left: The introduction of new, record-breaking size ships was not confined to the cruise divisions. In 1999 P&O ordered from Fincantieri the two largest passenger-car ferries ever built, which were constructed at the Marghera yard, near Venice. Designated as 'cruise ferries', the first of the 60,600-gross-ton pair, the *Pride of Rotterdam*, was laid down on 5 March 2000 and floated out of her building dock on 29 September 2000. The short building time was achieved by using modular construction techniques. Intended for the Hull to Rotterdam Beneluxhaven service of P&O North Sea Ferries, the *Pride of Rotterdam* entered service in April 2001, just over a year after construction commenced. She can accommodate 1,360 passengers, all in cabins with en suite facilities. Vehicle space has been provided for 250 private cars, 285 12m freight units and 125 double-stacked containers. Diesel engines driving twin screws give her a service speed of 22 knots. This view shows the *Pride of Rotterdam* being towed by tugs at Venice, revealing the unusual design of her forward end. The second picture (*below*) shows the *Pride of Rotterdam* from a more broadside angle. *Fincantieri / Mike Louagie*

Left: The second P&O North Sea Ferries mega-ferry, the *Pride of Hull*, is shown here in the building dock at Marghera, Venice, prior to being floated out. The bulbous bow is a striking feature of the underwater hull. Her keel was laid immediately after the 'launch' of her sister, the *Pride of Rotterdam*. These super-ferries, operating the overnight crossing, have been provided with extensive passenger facilities — a Sky Lounge on the top deck, a show lounge, an *à la carte* restaurant, a buffet restaurant and a café. There is also a shopping arcade. The *Pride of Hull*, like her sister-ship, has dimensions of 707ft (215.5m) length overall and 105ft (32.0m) beam. With the *Norsea* and *Norsun*, plus the older, stretched *Norland* and *Norstar*, the introduction of the *Pride of Rotterdam*, followed by the *Pride of Hull* in December 2001, brings the P&O North Sea Ferries fleet strength to six first-rate vessels. *P&O North Sea Ferries*

Overleaf: The *Pride of Hull* is seen at Beneluxhaven in Rotterdam's Europort, after she had entered service on the overnight service from Hull. *Mike Louagie*

Above: The latest P&O ship to enter service is the 110,000-gross-ton *Star Princess,* third of the 'Grand Princess' class, which made her inaugural sailing in January 2002. And she is certainly not the last new vessel of the current round of construction. Another four to five ships, representing a massive 555,000 gross tons and 15,000 passenger berths, are either under construction or on order for delivery by 2005. There is the already mentioned super cruise ship for P&O Cruises, which may or may not come to fruition, plus four new giants for Princess Cruises — the *Coral Princess* and *Island Princess,* of similar proportions, from Chantiers de L'Atlantique, St Nazaire, and the even larger *Diamond Princess* and *Sapphire Princess* from Mitsubishi Heavy Industries, Japan. Collectively, they are destined to reinforce the P&O Group's position as one of the lead players in the world's cruise industry. By 2004, the Princess Cruises fleet alone will have a total of 30,000 berths, accommodating at full occupancy some 1.5 million passengers per year. *Fincantieri*

Left: The bow-on view reveals the enormous breadth of the *Star Princess's* navigating bridge structure, extending well beyond the sides of her hull. *Fincantieri*